ARE YOU ACTUALLY GOING TO BE PROLIFIC OR JUST MAKE EXCUSES?

A very aggressive guide to fast writing, publishing, and being a professional writer.

BRANDON SCOTT

*For those who want to make art their life.
For those who respect art for its power, majesty, and transformative influence.
For those who are ready to begin.*

Copyright © 2020 by Brandon Scott

All rights reserved.

No part of this publication may be reproduced in any form or by any means whatsoever without the prior written permission of the author except in the case of brief quotations embodied in critical articles or reviews.

Contents

Prelude 1: 1

What to expect from this book, and why it might not be for me? 1

Prelude 2: 3

How to use this second book. 3

The New World of Books 5

The Market as It Is, Not as We Want It to Be 9

The Piecemeal Author Is an Author Without Branding .12

Assignment 1: 15

The Idea Mill 18

What Actually Makes for a Good Book Idea 20

The Book That Fascinates You 27

Assignment 2: 29

The Absolute Worst Thing You Can Do When You Want to Write Fast 36

Sprinting to Writing Victory 40

I Swear Your Art Will Be Okay 43

Some Very Harsh Numbers 45

Find the Next Sentence 48

The Outlining Exception 50

Assignment 3:	52
Editors	55
Self-Editing Mindset	57
Software and Computer Things	59
Your Ear is A Better Editor Than Your Eyes	61
The Fear of The Publish	64
Assignment 4:	66
My Own Personal Writer's Block	72
Keep Down the Cost	74
Getting Stuff Off Your Plate	77
The Stuff in The Book You Probably Forgot to Write	79
Assignment 5:	81
Art Is Subjective and People Like Different Stuff	84
Assignment 6 and Beyond:	86
About the Author	91

Prelude 1:

WHAT TO EXPECT FROM THIS BOOK, AND WHY IT MIGHT NOT BE FOR ME?

Hello, hi, and howdy. The name is Brandon Scott, and I did not expect to be writing another book on this subject so soon. But people seem to like the first book, and I have far more to tell on the subject of writing. There's a lot more to being an author, and to being creative in the modern world.

So, here we are again.

But, before I continue, before we get into the weeds, let's set some things straight, manage expectations, and clarify what exactly you are reading right now.

This book is a book for the serious writer. It is not meant for the hobbyist. It is not for the wishy-washy. It will have no patience for those so fond of talking about their dreams of being a pro-writer but are not willing to work.

If you are not prepared to sit down and *work,* then I will not be able to do a damn thing for you. You may as well refund this book right now or donate it to a library or something—no sense wasting paper.

If you are still here, I hope you are ready.

And, if you are still here, I need to clarify something:

I am not here to stroke your ego or assure you. This is *not* a motivational book. My previous book was full of motivation because new authors need it. To get people going, you need to support them. But this book is for people wanting to do this as a side-hustle or even a full job. This will not be easy or even fun all the time. This is not something you can do "around your busy schedule" or "just on the weekends."

This is serious work. This is *very* serious work. If you've read my previous book, then you know why. Artists are some of the most important people on the planet. It is my honor to make them and make them produce good work.

I will be giving you tools that will allow you to be a multi-series author in a *single year*. They are proven, effective, and explosive.

So, take them seriously.

Prelude 2:

HOW TO USE THIS SECOND BOOK.

Okay, here's how this book will be structured. Here's how it will work.

The first thing of note is this book is a sequel to another book I wrote called *Are You Actually Going To Write A Book or Just Talk About It?: An Aggressive Guide To Writing, Creativity, and Actually Getting Things Done.* I will expand and reiterate on points covered there. I may even repeat myself.

That's because this book needs to be a toolkit that someone could feasibly read without reading the first one. It may also reiterate because truth and workable methods will sound the same or similar no matter how it's said.

Lies and fancy have variations. The truth will always ring with the same tune.

So, I'm sorry if you feel like I'm wasting your time in places—just know that I will only repeat things vital to remember.

Now, as to the rules of this book, they are, as they always will be:

1. I will give you references to read first. I expect you to read them in the order presented. I expect you to check online or in a dictionary if you do not understand a word, a term, or a slang phrase.

2. I will then give you an assignment. You are to do that assignment to the best of your abilities. Do not read past them to the references beyond until you have done them, or I otherwise say so. I repeat: *Do the assignment I give before you even turn the fucking page to the next thing unless I tell you otherwise.*

3. You are not me, and I am not you. These methods work, I know they work, and they are based on experience. However, if following me to the letter seems not the most helpful way to do something, then you can interpret me to your needs. But if you do that and it does not go as I say it will—then you can't blame me. I am giving you these tools, these ideas, to help you, and to make you a prolific author. So, trust me, eh?

Okay, that's all. That's my prelude. We have a lot to go over for this, so let's begin. Read up to assignment one.

THE NEW WORLD OF BOOKS

Regardless of the perception that people may have about it, books are not a dying medium. They are thriving and building people's careers. You may not see them, but there are individuals out there who are not famous, are not well-known, and making shit tons of money. I'm talking thousands a month. I'm talking *livable* wages.

Yeah, a lot are romance writers, but, still, there is and has been a market for books, full of customers, that you simply do not see. I didn't see them either until I knew where to look.

But this resurgence, as far as I understand it, is because of the cash cow that is the binge reader. Some people are ready and willing to pay for cheap books, then read them in a day, then buy another.

A feverish book-hungry can easily eat through an author's back catalog and give them a sales boost that is not unsubstantial.

Multiply this by hundreds of thousands of people, and those numbers I mentioned are not so strange anymore.

That's how this works.

That's how you win as an author.

So, then, comes the implications, and why you need to think with this.

We are not living in a world where the average writer can pump out one book after years and survive. There's no releasing one masterpiece and becoming a bestseller and sitting pretty on that income.

That's not to say it does not happen. It does, and it will. But it's not a reliable way for the average author or professional writer. It's not worth trying, because the wasted time is deadly.

And I hate to do this and say this to people who do not like mass writing, but that perfectionist method is not the method of work, of career, of a job as a writer.

If you are a hobbyist, then fine. Go ahead. If you are not interested in being widely read, or making money at this, then fine. Toil on your masterpiece all you want.

But for the rest of us, you need to do this:

You need to write and publish fast. Not even a book a year is likely to cut it anymore. This is a world where people watch an entire television series in a day and then want another. This is a world where YouTubers have to make a video a week to even attempt to survive, and some a lot more videos than that.

It's a world where you have to make constantly, and where quality does not matter as much as quantity.

I'm not saying to pump out bad books, but you do not have the luxury of satisfaction or even experimentation anymore.

You need to write fast, you need to write a series, and you need to release a book once a month, if not more.

And it will only get more fast-paced, more intense, as authors embrace this mindset and fill up everywhere that they possibly can.

I am no different, and you can't be either. Your backlist makes you money, your series makes you money. Releasing new content is the only way to keep attention on your work. For our purposes, and the mindset we need, we must think that the world does not care about anything but the recently made. It does not care about anything more than a month old.

That may sound cruel. That may sound callous. That may hurt your heart as an artist…

But it's the truth. There is no changing it. People can fight against it all they want, but art is influenced by economics more than anyone would care to admit. This is the world we are living in, and I cannot imagine the words I type now becoming anything else but more and more true.

So, accept that. You can take a minute to breathe—but you must accept it.

Then be prepared for more work than you imagined, and for the mystique of being an author to flake away in the searing wind of modern-day publishing.

Be prepared to produce words on a scale that's mind-numbing to consider.

THE MARKET AS IT IS, NOT AS WE WANT IT TO BE

Readers have expectations, and if you do not meet them, then you will have a problem as a professional.

If you are an experimental writer, a cross-genre writer, then you need to understand something pertinent. You must grasp that for those pursuits to work towards your career, you need to balance it with things expected and things anticipated.

Readers, despite what they might say, do not want to be surprised. They are not looking for real shocks, not really. They love a good twist, but not a wild twist. Discovering who the real father was in a romance novel is not the same as a sudden introduction of aliens into an otherwise contemporary coming-of-age story. You need to know that going in and before you type a single word.

Let me clarify this: you need to follow a genre, and you need to follow the wants and desires of your readers.

You need to have a happy ending. You need to use tropes and make them not deviate too much. You need to not kill an animal character or hurt young characters unless that is relevant to your genre.

Do not break these rules, or, if you do, then don't break them all the time. Release five books that follow these ideas, and then one for creative freedom where you can go your own way. Just don't expect that one to be your bestseller.

I know this idea may make you squirm—it makes me squirm. I'm a contrarian, but I cannot argue with the backlash against stories that do not follow a three-act structure. I cannot undo that anger when the couple does not get together at the end of the story. The disgust from an author suddenly murdering a character without warning.

Look, I get you maybe saw something like that done in a movie or show you liked. You're not them. That was likely made by someone with a lot of practice, and industry wisdom, and with a lot of forethought.

You should not be attempting to do something like that without over ten books under your belt.

You do not have the practice.

And you need it before you're going to alter rules and try to break out of tropes. You need an established audience.

I'm sorry that it is this way, but that's just the way it is.

And you can rebel against me, not listen to this point, and think you'll be the one to break the mold.

And maybe you'll succeed. But the odds are against you, and writing books is a dream job, so why risk it more than you need to?

Don't worry, there will be plenty of chances to write cool plots, to try stuff you never have before. You'll be amazed at what you are allowed to do within the constraints of genre. It's not all doom and gloom, but there are rules, and you do need to follow them.

THE PIECEMEAL AUTHOR IS AN AUTHOR WITHOUT BRANDING

Not to make you feel too pigeonholed, but before you begin insane writing output, you need to be clear about who you are as an author. This is important for marketing reasons, and for the cultivation of fans, and for knowing what you will need to do to travel this path.

You need to pick a genre and then stick to your genre, or within connecting avenues.

Stephen King is a horror writer, and we all know that. We know if we are reading a book by him, then horror is what we should expect. That's branding, and it is powerful.

Want horror? You have a name on your tongue already.

However, if you write a romance novel, then a high fantasy book, perhaps dabble in westerns, you are going to lose that mental real estate. You will also chop up your potential to absolute ribbons.

Because you will lose any chance of getting readers to hop books. Yeah, your audience may like you, but they will not go read a whole new genre outside of their comfort zone just because it's you.

Now, that's not to say you are stuck. Some genres are rather flexible, and you can play within some bounds.

You can't hop genres within the same series, but, outside of that, you can go to any genre that is a subgenre of your main. A lot of genres are okay lumped together.

Now, this is somewhat my own opinion and not based on experience but think about if you heard that Stephen King wrote a romance book. That would be jarring—and you would only consider reading it out of novelty.

Now consider he had written a dark murder mystery story—that's not so hard to grasp. It's connected enough to the genre, so long as the killer is suitably violent. Or dark fantasy, so long as it was crunchy enough with its darkness.

Science fiction authors can usually get away with some fantasy writing. Viking romance authors can *probably* get away with some renaissance era romance.

Now, of all the chapters, this is the one I have the least authority to speak on, as I am guilty of hopping genres. But I can confirm that I do have a segmented readership. It is costing me readers and is making me have to divert my energy to advertising to different types of readers.

I can confirm it is a bad idea, and that it is detrimental. I can also confirm that authors who do not do this are much, much better off because they picked a genre and stuck with it.

So, yeah, before you churn out words, consider it, and think about who you are and what your strengths as a storyteller are. Pick a genre you love and would not mind staying in for a long time.

You will eventually get to expand but be prepared to commit to at least a year of one genre. Commit to writing at least an entire series.

You want to become known as a "genre author." So, play within and respect your genre, and it will reward you.

Assignment 1:

I realize that I will be telling you to do a fair bit before you start writing books. That is only to make sure that it all goes smoothly for you when you do. There's no sense in not stretching before the marathon.

It would be irresponsible to start you with nothing to guide you. So, bear with a few assignments and quite a few lessons before you go off and become a prolific author. It is necessary work.

If most people could just become prolific right out of the gate, then we would see it all the time, yeah?

So, let start with something a little easier:

1. Look over your collection of books. If you do not have one, mentally go through the stories you have read, or watched, or listened to. Pay the most attention to ones that stand out as important to your life. This should not be hard. If you are having trouble recalling the details of a book, then it is not the right book for this step.

2. Notice the prevailing genre. There will be outliers, but of the books you recall instinctually, what genre are they mostly? Did you read science fiction by the truckload, or were you raised on a steady diet of contemporary stories with young adult characters who fall in love? Dig deep here

and notice the trends of the stories. Did they feature a lot of violence, a lot of romantic scenes? What scenes affected you the most? Was it character deaths or long monologs? You can write this down, I suppose, to help figure it out, but it's better if its stuff you would never need a note to recall.

3. If needed, research these books, these tropes, or situations, and find the technical term for the subgenre. If you have no idea what I mean by this or think that genres aren't that narrow or specific, then go look online. Search for the term "cozy mysteries" and then do the same with the term "hard-boiled crime fiction." These are both technically in the same genre, but just look at the glaring differences between them.

4. Learn your genre of choice. Learn its name, it's even narrower variations, and who is writing in that genre. Discover at least five famous books/movies/plays in that genre. Watch them or read them. Likely, you already have seen at least one of them. This is one of the few times I will give you an assignment that is not writing, so do enjoy it. It is homework, and you are working—but it is the last time you will get to be this passive.

5. Think of yourself, refer to yourself, and operate with yourself as an author of that genre. If you

feel the need, you can even find craft books on a specific genre.

Now, this step may come as a shock to you. You may be surprised at what you find, and, sadly, it may not coincide with the genre or type of book you wanted to write. You may be a fan of one thing and a writer of another.

This is an unfortunate situation that can happen and has only a few options. One choice is you need to rapidly get as dedicatedly familiar with your preferred genre to write in as you are with your natural reading preferences. Otherwise, switch gears and write the genre you know and have an ingrained understanding of, abandoning those other stories until a later day.

That's your choice, but you do need to make it to get anywhere. If you do switch, then you need to do the above steps for what you switched to.

Once you have that all sorted out, and have done these steps, then you can read unto the next part. But not sooner. I want you to plan to be within a genre before you start the mental process of preparing to write books.

THE IDEA MILL

For the new writer, there are too many ideas in their head. They are plagued by too many stories they want to tell. Sometimes this is a powerful distraction that can make them start and never finish a lot of books.

And that's a different sort of problem.

But for us, for the people writing a lot of books, we will, really, and surprisingly, run out of things we want to write about.

You can exhaust ideas and characters if you write enough.

It may creep unto you slowly, it may suddenly be a wall, but I want it to be clear that you will someday face this problem. It might be better if I tell you how to handle that now rather than when you're deep into the thick of it.

So, the secret to handling this issue is that you need to live life.

It is that simple.

Imagination is not sprung from the ether. Your life and your passions and your days and days are feeding it.

The term "write what you know" gets bandied about a lot. It might seem cliché, but how to make it not a problem is to make sure you've lived a lot of life.

And I know you're an introvert, likely. You may not do "that kind of living" as much as others—but whoever said you had to go do what party animals do?

I said simply that you need to experience the world. Whatever that means for you, and whatever is fun for you.

Do you like unique foods? Cool! Make your character like those dishes. Then, in your real life, go have more unique foods.

When you write books, there might be a feeling you are a slave to your stories. There is a degree of dedication needed, that is true, but that does not mean you shouldn't be taking breaks to go do fun, interesting, or fascinating things.

Research holes—during *free time*—is not a bad idea. Experience other cultures, weird diseases, plant life, holidays you've never heard of before, and so many other compelling topics.

This is the food of your stories, and just because you are now using what life you've lived before doesn't mean you stop gathering new stuff.

You will run out, so keep giving it new fuel.

WHAT ACTUALLY MAKES FOR A GOOD BOOK IDEA

In the modern-day, with modern storytelling and trope savvy audiences, you can't get away with just telling something that you think would be cool to tell. That's not enough anymore—so it seems relevant to go over what kind of ideas will make for a writeable, readable, and marketable book.

The usual mindset on this is that to have a good story, you need an interesting character who wants something interesting. Or, at the very least, one aspect of your story needs to be interesting. You can have an everyman pursue a dinosaur bride or desire to drink the world's first intelligent cup of chicken broth and it *will* come out "interesting."

But that's not getting across the full breadth of a good premise. Instead, before you begin a book in your genre, I suggest you work out four pivotal things to determine whether a story will be worth the time to write.

Those four things are:

1. An interesting character
2. An interesting goal
3. A gimmick
4. A prevailing mood or tone

Let's work them through, shall we?

An Interesting Character:

What makes a person interesting? Much has been written on the subject, and frankly this book is not the craft book to dive deep—there are other, better books for such things. We could go into passive characters or reactive characters or characters with agency, but that's more subjective than people seem to think it is. Instead, we're going to bare bones this shit.

An interesting person in a story is memorable in some way, is someone we can have a strong emotional reaction to (good or bad) and does something in the story.

Oh yeah, that's broad, arguable, and maybe too basic. But some characters are just a bunch of cool visual aspects and one-liners and very shallow personality traits and are *beloved*. Simple is not inherently bad. If they keep the story interesting, and we are interested in them, they are a character worth reading.

Sure, you can write pages and pages of backstory and explore their values and habits and stuff—but you don't have to, not really. Not if it doesn't matter to their story.

Just think of someone who would be interesting to follow along for an adventure or a day or a trip and you've got the marrow of a book.

<u>An Interesting Goal:</u>

Some goals are inherently interesting and easy to get behind. Most people know what it's like to want to feel safe, to feel loved, to find a romantic partner, to not have financial worries anymore, or to help someone they love.

That's one option: Have a character with a goal that a real person might have or likely will have. You've got a chance for instant empathy for the character if you go that route.

The other option is a goal so very specific or bombastic or exciting that it's also interesting. You can be too broad with this. No one cares about "saving the world" much anymore. It's flat and obvious. Go a little more detailed.

How about fixing a *broken* world? Or exploring a new one to escape a bad world?

If that doesn't appeal to you, there are other paths to this option. You can also go very specific or even very goofy. How about a character that will go against the odds for something as simple as a taco? That's specific, strange, and interesting all by itself.

It also ties right into the next part—the gimmick—because the two are sometimes the same and sometimes distinct.

So, let's talk about that now.

A Gimmick:

The word "gimmick" has such a negative perception. I don't mean it that way—I mean something about your story that makes it seem interesting in a way that you could say in a sentence.

One template for this is "it's like (usually expected trope or plot concept), but (widely divergent or off-kilter concept)." That's not the only template, but it's one that's easy to grasp.

Gimmicks do not have to be unique; they just have to be inherently fun or interesting. Science fiction and fantasy books have an easy time hitting this concept.

For instance, the "time loop" gimmick. Yeah, you know of it because of *Groundhog's Day*, but it's a strong gimmick that's fun to play with and will remain fun to play with for a while.

That movie has such a killer gimmick you can't help but be sucked in just by hearing about it.

Now, certain gimmicks are specifically loved by different people. Some people just want a preferred gimmick anywhere they can get it. And, honestly, if you have a gimmick that is your shit, then go for it. You will get across your love of that premise, so long as you aren't ripping off the story that did it first.

Finding a gimmick isn't always easy, however, depending on genre. Despite what impression I may give off, I have read a lot of romance novels, and they are going wild over there with what gimmicks they are trying. They have to. Gimmicks are a strong way to gather interest and to differentiate yourself from the other stories in your genre.

My only warning is that gimmicks must not be pointless. They must not exist for the sole reason to have one.

Your gimmick needs to be intrinsic to the tale, and how it is presented. Imagine if *Groundhog's Day* literally had a single time loop and then didn't do it again and never mentioned it again? That would be a terrible movie and you would feel cheated.

Your gimmick is a promise, and I would honestly like the term de-stigmatized because of it.

If you can find a new gimmick, one not done a ton yet, then you are sitting on a storytelling goldmine. That's hard to do, though, so don't be afraid to simply tweak existing gimmicks.

Make your gimmick your own but understand that the "interesting premise" is real power in storytelling and marketing. It's sometimes enough to get someone to make a purchase just by hearing about it.

A Prevailing Mood or Theme:

A story stuck in one mood is not interesting. But, there's usually an underlying emotion to the story you are writing, and it helps a lot to know what it is. Dystopian Satire stories are typically bleak or depressing, whereas Romance is usually more casual or emotionally dramatic.

Except when they are not.

Your mood or theme can be a gimmick. If you want to write a sour, bitter, depressing romance novel, then your mood *is* a gimmick. Though I would not recommend that one specifically.

Regardless of your choice, though moments can break the mood, you need to hold to a mood to construct a plot. If you are going for sad, then you will not structure your plot to be full of shenanigans. If you want happy stories, then maybe cut back on the disemboweling scenes.

You get my point here.

The mood can help inform your storyline, and it is relevant to think with as your working.

These, put together, and made to work with each other, will leave you with a cohesive book concept you can feasibly write and then sell.

But that does not mean you should be writing this down as your thinking about it.

Put that notepad away, my studious reader. Shred that note.

Because there's one more part to this, and it deserves its own page(s).

THE BOOK THAT FASCINATES YOU

The book you should write should not leave your mind.

It should claw at you to write it, make you ponder it, imagine it, and wonder about it.

I don't mean this in a spurt of short-term excitement.

No.

I mean that the book you should write should be dreamed up, then not started for an entire month.

Yes, a month.

Let me explain. Ideas for books that appear suddenly in someone's head are often shallow.

Sometimes, yes, great book ideas come in seconds and are golden glittery things.

But most aren't and most won't be.

So, the true way to test it is to *not write it down*. Don't scrawl it in a notebook or get it on some recording for your future consideration.

If a story is good, then it can survive in your memory. If a story has potential, it can survive on your interest alone. A good story will make it to the page with no way to stay in existence except personal fascination for an entire month.

If the story cannot last through the challenge, then it would not be something you were going to particularly enjoy writing.

And, yeah, this is a harsh way to do it. A method that may feel like you'll lose something great or brilliant.

But my response to you is: if it's such a good idea, such an enduringly shiny bit of storytelling majesty, then why would you forget it?

If you, *the author*, can forget about it that easily, then what hope would the buying public have?

So, take it from me. Sit on an idea for a month, an entire month, thirty fucking days, with no notes, no memorization help, and no tangible way to hold on to it. If you still remember it enough to be excited about it, then be prepared to *write* that sucker.

Because you just found a good book idea.

Assignment 2:

This is a tricky one (and a long one). I do not expect you to wait an entire month before you do the thing this book is made to teach. No one would do that anyway, so why would I ask?

I will, later, go into how you will incorporate the one-month-book-idea concept into your actual schedule as an author. Meanwhile, I'll give you an assignment to begin the process of your prolific life.

This step is onetime and is not my usual advice. It will kind of mess up the math and the rhythm that I will instill for the rest of the assignments. But, the purpose of this is to jump into the writing path and publishing path faster. We have to start somewhere.

If, later, you find you fell out of the prolific mindset and routine, then refer to this assignment, as it is tailored for that situation and almost nothing else.

So, to begin, without a month lead-in for idea cultivation, we'll start with this:

1. Come up with a simple story idea. Not short-story simple, but something that comes fully formed in one go. If you can say it in a single sentence without a "but" or a "however" or is something you could imagine filling the plot of a one-hour

episode of a show, then you're in the right ballpark.

2. Make a folder (not a file, an entire folder) on your computer, or get a real manilla folder, or buy a notebook and mark it. Some permanent markers may be in order, but I understand if you don't want to mar something pretty like an artistic notebook.

3. Create a file or segmented section to be labeled "Word Bible" or "Story Bible" or "Story Guide." Whichever feels like the most intuitive version of that phrasing.

4. In that section, note down your main character's first, last, and if wanted, middle name. You'll also need their basic physical description (the minimum you need is eye color, hair color, age, and a vague notion of height and build). Now determine their goal—as we've discussed. Write it as a sentence they might say out loud. If your character would say it as "I want to fucking kill the bastard who murdered my parents," or "Justice must be served! It is the will of the Lord for this sinner to perish," then you've already got a strong personality baseline.

5. Repeat for any characters you also will explore in this story. Don't take too long on this step—you need not go too deep. If a character is not very

important to the story, then just do the physical description and their name.

6. Below that write down the name of the location(s) where the story is taking place and any very basic information about the location you would need to know. You need not get complicated. Unnecessary worldbuilding is a massive way to waste time and not write the actual story.

7. If your story contains any magical items, weird diseases, spells, or made-up brands or websites, then note them down. Include a very brief description of what it is or what it does. Again, do not go deep. DO NOT OVERDO THIS.

8. Next, make a file called "Outline." You can have more fun with this name, but, like, that's just another way to procrastinate.

9. Note: this is not the numbers I will tell you to do later. This way of doing it is specifically for this unique step. However, for now, you will use a spreadsheet or lined paper or similar to create 30 lines. No more, no less.

10. These will be your chapters. On each line, in a single phrase or sentence, write down one basic plot event. Something short and simple. Something like "main character discovers he's got the power to talk to animals."

11. Fill in all thirty with basic plot progression. This is where you will plan how the story will go and how it will end. You do not need to fill them in order. It may help to do the first and last ones to begin, then fill in the rest of them. I will repeat this aspect: you need not come up with much per line.

12. Create a subfolder (a folder within the main folder, for those of us not as tech-savvy) with the name of your book. Yes, you have to come up with a title right now, right away, and before you write the story. It's hard to explain why, but this is an important part of making the goal real, and the story tangible. A bit of advice for your title: I recommend something that is more than one word. One-word titles are very generic unless you can find one that's off the beaten path or so blunt that it's hard to ignore. Your main character's name is also a generic choice, and a bad one unless your main character has a unique name. Instead, aim for something around 2-7 words that is memorable and easy to say. You can also go for a long title, but then it needs to be so jarring or humorous or off-kilter that it's hard not to read the entire sentence. The length of your title, amazingly, is a signifier of tone and genre, so you do need to pay attention to that.

13. Okay, here's the actual writing. I promise the prep work you just did will make it easier to go into the

story. To start, you will make one file in your Book Title sub-folder and give it the name "Chapter 1" followed by these symbols "—" and then the name of the chapter, if you want to give each chapter its own name. Only make a file right before you are writing that chapter. Give each chapter its own separate file. Make sure to back up these files to cloud storage or an external hard drive or something similar.

14. *Every single day* you will write one of those thirty chapters. Each is going to be no less than 500 words, and ideally will not be much more than that either. In one sitting, in one day, you will write a chapter, and you will keep it within a small word count. This is important training for many reasons.

15. End every single chapter on something that pushes the reader to read the next chapter. Something ominous, something jarring, something teasing of what happens next. You can also do an actual cliffhanger. It doesn't matter which one, it's your choice, but you need to *never* put a chapter ending that feels like a comfortable place to pause. In this one instance, in this one way, you will be operating under the asshole assumption that you do not care about your readers' schedules. You are actively gunning to make something so compelling that it makes

people late to a meeting because they cannot stand to stop reading anywhere in the book.

16. As you write these chapters, pay attention to what other ideas are sparking in your head. There are likely ideas you had to abandon in the outlining of your book. Take a look at them as you go and begin planning—but do not record anything relating to—another book, another idea, which will be the next book you'll write.

Okay... that was a lot. And I'm sorry to front-load you with so many instructions. This is a short book, and you and I do not have the time to tiptoe around what we're doing here. I am trusting you to read through that slog of steps and do them.

Also, and here's the tough love bit again: this is the start of being a pro-author. This is the normal work but made easier. If you are already reeling from this task, then you are going to need to go read my last book and build up to this one.

I'm asking you now: do you have a genuine desire to do the work and live the life?

Are you just in it because it seems cool and like it's an easy way to make money?

It's not.

Go work in real estate or become a retail manager if money is all you're after.

This is what it's actually like. Sorry to break that to you.

As to the real writers, let's get going forward now. Because this step is me buying time and starting you off small—as you've likely already figured.

So you're ready when you get there, you may read ahead to the next assignment. Don't read the actual assignment. This is only so you can go right into the next step as soon as you finish writing your first book.

I will also be going over some methods and mindset changes for writing large amounts each day, so it should help you in that way. In some cases, I'll be reusing old articles I've written on the subject outside this book

THE ABSOLUTE WORST THING YOU CAN DO WHEN YOU WANT TO WRITE FAST

I have a question for you: are you a writer or an editor? Do you know the definition of each word? Have you checked?

Go check.

Does it say anywhere that a writer is an editor?

No? Good. *Then stop fucking doing it!* For the love of God, why are you trying to edit as you are being a writer?

And I hear you say you are both, that you will edit your writing, so you are both a writer and an editor.

Yeah, okay, fine. But stop being both simultaneously. They are different jobs. If you worked two jobs and those jobs were to be a waitress and then somewhere else you were a chef, would you ever try to do both at the same time?

That's a recipe for spilling food or burning someone's dish.

No, it's just stupid to try, and it's also the reason most people don't write fast enough. They reread what they are writing as they write. They stop and play with the same sentence forever and then only write like a paragraph or two during an entire hour.

It's easier to be disciplined and get writing momentum going if you are not stepping all over your efforts.

Being a writer and editor are separate tasks and should be done at different times.

The mindsets are different as are the intentions.

So, when you write, when you put fingers to keys, the only thing you may change as you are typing it is typos. And that's only because reading back something with typos is needlessly confusing.

You just type and type and type and do not look back. Fill the page with words, no matter how shitty. Fill it so you can edit something that exists.

Despite what I just said, you might still have the idea that you can do both. The logic might go "once I've finished writing, I will have a perfectly complete manuscript and can move straight to publishing."

It feels efficient, right?

Uh… no.

That's not how that works. It's not a perfect analogy but imagine if you decorated a cake with icing and little figures and stuff *before you had put the batter in the oven.*

You'd just need to remove it all and maybe even start over with the cake.

Look, I know it might feel painful to produce bad words. They may even feel like something sour sitting in your stomach—but you will fix them later. You *have* to fix them *later*. You don't know enough about the book you, notably, haven't *finished writing*, to figure out how to edit it. No outline can mirror a finished product enough to assure that you can skip the raw writing step.

No one needs to see your shitty words. That's fine. They will see what you fixed later.

I cannot stress this enough. I cannot fail to repeat it enough: just write, do not edit as you do, and then fix it later.

Every other way will cause slower writing and stifled creativity.

Maybe someone out there works the other way, but why would you mess with a method I can guarantee will make you write faster? Why would you not just do the thing that works and lets you write in a fun way?

Writing, just writing, is like letting the imagination out of your head. It's like dreaming in words.

It's magical.

An editor's job is to take dreams and put it into reality. It's a noble and needed job for readers. Readers aren't in the head of the writer, and thus words need a medium even beyond the creator's own efforts to understand it.

Writers can edit their work; they often need to do so. But, when being an editor, you need to think and act and have the priorities of an editor. That's a different job.

So, let the writer-you do what it does best. Then, when it is the time to do it, let the editor-you do their job.

Don't get in your way. There's no point to it.

SPRINTING TO WRITING VICTORY

I write fast as it is. That's a brag—I think I earned it. I've written more than a million words and I'm still in my twenties. That's probably worth some credit.

But even I was not prepared for how effective writing sprints are for me.

Like, these things are absurd.

A bit of backstory. I've been dealing with the problem of not publishing fast enough to get a good backlist and thus better book sales. I just haven't been that fast at editing to make it possible. And I would read from these authors who somehow get out books at a rate like one every few weeks.

That sounded insane. And everything I did to figure what shortcut they must be using found no shortcuts. These were 200+ page books, fully edited, with covers and everything.

And that made me sad for a while because I couldn't fathom coming that close to speeds like that.

But then I learned (still learning to actually use) the magic bullet to at least write that fast. I've yet to master the editing part.

And this method may not work if you're not already a writer with some practice under your belt. It feels like it might be too intense if you don't have the practice and experience telling tales.

But, if you are a writer who has written for a while, you've got to try this. I'm averaging over 1000 words a day in less than a half-hour with this method.

I did the math, and if I used this method for even an hour a day, I would have written a 90,000-word novel (350 or so pages) a month. A *month*.

I had to read three books on related subjects to figure this much out:

1. You need a *detailed* chapter-by-chapter outline and world bible. You can only write fast because you don't have to think too hard about your plot while you're doing it. You can "pants" this, but it's slower.

2. You need essentially a locked away, quiet, Wi-Fi-free zone. Or to make a place like that. Turn off your phone, seal the doors, and make sure you don't and won't need to pee—because you will be glued to your chair.

3. Have a clock with a timer on it that works without the internet or Wi-Fi. Both your computer and your smartphone should be able to do this.

4. Dim the lights or turn them off so everything but the screen and the words are in shadows or fuzzy to the eye. I am easily distracted. If you are too, this can help limit anything that might slow you down.

5. Get a saved music playlist that contains songs with no lyrics and no intense instrumentation. Just something to drown out random sounds but not too interesting as to be distracting.

6. Set a timer for twenty-five minutes, note your start time, and just pedal to the metal write without self-editing or even thinking back on what you just wrote. Create new chapters as you go if needed and stop when the timer stops. I find being amid a scene makes it more tempting to go back to writing the next time.

7. Note down all of what you did, every time, in one place. You'll have redundant information but note it all down.

This could change your path as an author and a writer. I have never come across a speed-writing method that works as well as this simple idea of removing distractions and doing it for a very defined set of time.

Seriously, get on this shit.

I SWEAR YOUR ART WILL BE OKAY

Toiling away at your latest art project can take longer than it needs to take.

Let me repeat that: you can make art faster.

But how? Well, many artists and creators can get out creations faster if they simply let go of something: their need for it to be perfect.

Because, uh, just so you know: no art is perfect. Art is made to communicate with someone's soul, even if it's only the creators. And, for anything to be connecting with someone, it must fail to do so with others.

No art is universal. Not everyone in the world likes bacon or ice cream or milk chocolate. You think a subjective exploration of a communication dreamed up by a human mind will have a chance at blanket acceptance and praise?

No, of course not. And it's ridiculous to hold yourself to that standard.

So, don't. Get it good *enough*.

I don't mean be lazy, or slack off, or ship out stuff that's the minimum of what you can do. I mean stop at the point you can't help but tweak this or that. I mean at the stage where you wonder if the character, in one scene and one scene only, "strode" across the room or "walked," it's best to decide and just move on with your life.

Get something out the door. Give art to the world.

It needs it.

Not releasing art when it's ready is holding it back from people who would want it.

Look, I get it: I've pondered a single word in a transition sentence (is "they walked to the house" enough?!) for minutes at a time while editing. But I need to remember that I am the only one in the world who is going to care. So long as I am improving at my art, I will not like my creations a year from now anyway.

So, it's not so big a deal.

Get your art to a decent place, not second-guess so much, and move towards production and improvement and *new projects*.

The first book you write, no matter how much you toil at it, will not be your best book.

Take the edge off and make cool shit.

SOME VERY HARSH NUMBERS

Time for a reality check that will not be fun but will be rather insightful and useful. I'm not a big fan of math, and, honestly, by the end of reading this you might not be either—but at least you'll know what you're dealing with.

So, a fairly well-known and fairly effective path to authorship success is to write and release a book a month, and to promote it through a newsletter. That sounds nice, yeah? Well, you need to look over the numbers and see the implications to properly get how much this adds up to in your actual day.

Let's start with the word count. Inexperienced writers (and non-writers) often think of books in page count, but that's not a good way to do it. Pages vary by formatting and by cover size and by a lot of other factors. It has less than expected to do with the words put to paper, so there's no sense in using it as a baseline.

Instead, you need to think of books as a lot of words.

How many words? Well, it varies, but for our purposes let's say an average book is 70,000 words. That's a realistic number and is around the size you think of when you think of a normal paperback you'd get at a store.

I do need to note that genre determines size. High Fantasy skews longer, for instance. But, for our purposes, let's stick to 70,000.

Now, let's look at a month. Let's say a month is 28 days. That's the smallest a month gets, so it works out as a consistent number. If we write a book in 28 days, we will end up with a little extra time each year, which is also nice.

I assume you already see the math you have to do here and realize what that means for a daily word count. But, if you don't want to think it through or take out a calculator, here's the math:

70,000/28=2500.

If you must think of that in physical pages, then use 250 words=1 page as your baseline for visualizing the number. That's ten pages a day. That's 280 pages with our numbers—which, again, is more an estimation, but also not an unreal one.

Now, don't freak out too much. It *is* possible to write that much daily, and it is possible to do this in that allotted time. I also picked a slightly high word count to illustrate my point. I find 50,000-ish to be a lot more manageable of a number. You only need to write about 1800 a day for that.

But even that's a little rough, and also an odd number to go with—which makes it harder to think of as a goal.

This is why, after a lot of writing and testing and some very sleepy nights, I stumbled upon the number that feels manageable. It's doable even for someone who's only written one book before. It's a minimum that will get you where you need to go and will let you finish books at a good clip. A clip decent enough to make a dent in the publishing market.

But this is as low as you can go, and it is daily, and it is every single day, even weekends, even holidays. There are no sick days as a writer. There are no breaks at first.

You earn those after a few books under your belt.

And that number is 1500 words a day.

I cannot touch type. I am not as fast as some people, but even I can do 1500 in an hour. An hour and a half on a bad day.

That's a little more time than some people devote to workouts each day—and I'm sure the results of that speak for themselves.

As will this.

Writing 1500 words a day and writing slightly shorter books will allow you to confidently create book after book after book and become a prolific author. It is the grind, and it can be grueling, and it can be hard, but it is rewarding, and it will work.

The math checks out.

FIND THE NEXT SENTENCE

In the quest for the daily word count, there may come times where you are up late and tired. You may find yourself unable to think straight and considering not writing for the day.

That is *not* the solution. Letting yourself have one break, one day off, is the death of the rhythm, and must not be allowed to happen. It is tremendously damaging allowing procrastination to enter into writing a book.

But you can get rather tired and feel like you don't know where you are going with this whole thing. That does happen.

So, what is there to be done about it?

Find the next sentence.

One simple sentence, like a step toward the oasis on the horizon. One sentence until the next. Write a few dull or basic sentences to find where you are going and for you to find where you are.

Your characters will eventually take up the slack again, and let you continue.

Even if at first it is nonsense, you should eventually see where it is going.

You must have faith, even in the darkest moments, that this is how it works. Success is what will inevitably happen.

One word, then another. Whatever you can see next in the story fog: write that.

THE OUTLINING EXCEPTION

I am just making sure that you understand the technique for outlining. I've covered it before, in this book and the last. The basic concept still holds—I just need to make sure you understand the scaling that is needed for this.

You will still need to do an outline, with the spreadsheet or whatever it is—but with a much higher word count. You will be breaking down a 70,000 or more story into little chunks of 1500 bits, or even smaller.

The most important thing about an outline by chapter is to make sure that you can fill each one with what you need for the overall book-length.

If you are the type to not have a lot to say for each scene, then you need to make your outline a lot of little chunks. I find the 1500 way is by far the most efficient for getting the word count down, but I have experimented with other methods. There is an alternative tactic for writing long books I have found successful.

And this is the only time you will get me saying it. I will not reference it anywhere else in this book. I only recommend it if you find my other method to be too draining.

Instead of every chapter being 1500 words, and you write one a day, you write three 500-word chapters in the same day.

This method will make the plot move a lot faster and may result in you writing over 1500 words a day and in aggregate *a lot more than usual* over a few days. It's easy to go over into 600 words, for instance, when you need to cram an entire idea into a few pages.

It's also a good way to get a lot of cliffhangers into a story, if that is your style, and if that is your genre. Thrillers, for instance, would likely benefit from this method much more than epic fantasy.

Again, I don't recommend you go straight to this method—I set up this book with precise steps, after all—but I wanted you to have it if you need it.

So use it wisely, okay?

Assignment 3:

Oh, we are in the shit storm now, my reader. This is where the pedal meets the metal and the real workers are driven to the top and the rest dashed upon the rocks.

I hope you're ready for this.

You are about to enter a world where you are writing at a pace that's going to shock and startle you, or slowly kill you.

I'm only half being dramatic.

This is where that second book idea needs to come into existence, and where the pace and the rhythm will come into play.

Most steps you should already have an idea of. This should not be surprising to you. I'm also not going to be as detailed here, as you should already have a good idea of how to do these steps.

1. Do an Outline and World Bible for the second book you have been planning to write. The one that survived the idea grinder of an entire month. This should all be done in one night, one sitting, and does count toward your 1500 words. I repeat: You do not need to write anything more on the day you do this. Unless you write less than 1500 words of background detail, you're done for the

day. That should not happen though. It should not be that short of a document that you didn't. I said you could go too deep, but you can also not go deep enough.

2. The next day, whenever you can, write the first chapter of your new book. This should, ideally, be done in one sitting. Writing sprints do not always work, but they are an effective way to at least get into the beginning of a story. It's okay if you have to do the word count piecemeal throughout the day, but it's not the optimum choice. The focus and momentum of continuous writing gets the word count *going*. Distracted, broken writing is not quick writing.

3. After the first seven days of your new novel, you will be editing your previous book simultaneously. Yes, simultaneously. How else would you be able to publish every month? The only other option would be to write 3000 words a day for half a month and then edit the other half of the month. I don't recommend this because if you stop writing new words each day your rhythm will suffer. I know it seems daunting but get used to it as quick as you can. For this to work, you're going to be writing a new book while editing an old book pretty much at all times.

And that's it. Only, of course, it's not. Because I haven't given you any advice on how to edit at the same time as writing. That's what the next section is about.

But don't jump to it yet.

I do not want you to read the next section until the fifth or sixth day, the day right before you will need to edit. The first few days of writing your book should be devoted mentally, as much as possible, to just the book you're typing away at tirelessly.

You will need to learn to split your attention soon enough though, and that's difficult. However, it's the only way to maximize output and to keep throwing more gasoline on the publishing fire.

So, start on the steps, get into your second book, and then, after some time, go to your editing, and learn to juggle these chainsaws.

Don't worry, I have some advice.

EDITORS

Editors, good ones anyway, are not your enemy.

They are not out to hurt your art.

They are simply not directly connected to your creation and thus can see warts you do not see. A good editor can tell what should be coming from your story and help guide you towards it.

There are only two things in writing a book that need to cost a lot. They are the two most important things to get right.

The two things are making sure the book is readable and enjoyable and making sure the cover is good enough.

Ugly covers are *fucking inexcusable* and will ruin any chance of sales. But, if you have a good cover, and then the words beyond it are awful, then you'll have people refunding your book.

Further, an editor cannot save a shitty manuscript. Good writing takes practice and is a skill you must learn. You need to produce something the editor can do something with. So long as gold is there, no matter how buried, an editor can help drag it towards the light.

However, an editor is a professional and does not deserve your first draft. Don't bang out words and then just shoot it off to them and expect them to return with perfect prose.

Before an editor touches your work, you must learn to edit yourself.

There is no cheating at this. Learn grammar, learn the language you are writing in, and learn how to tell a story. No software, at least without some serious science fiction shit going on, will ever replace your ability to understand the context of *your* story. No program can yet deal with the strange and odd nature of human language and make changes that make sense in every instance.

Do the work, then get a human editor to help it further.

SELF-EDITING MINDSET

Self-editing is the art of disconnecting yourself from your own creations and being as merciless and cold with them as possible.

That's the simple and short of it.

But I will go further into what I mean.

When you are self-editing a book, you need to forget that you are the one who wrote it. I'm a professional movie and television critic, so this is especially easy for me. I just need to imagine my book is a piece of media that someone else made that I need to review.

If you can easily adopt this mindset, then you will have a much calmer time of it. If you can channel whatever nature you have as a moviegoer who pays a lot of attention to if there are plot holes or mistakes in a movie, then go hog-wild on your work.

Be you the editor—not you the writer.

They are, for our purposes, different people, with no relation or opinion of the other. The guy who wrote this manuscript was from several hundred' miles away in some town you've never heard of before.

It's impersonal, cold, and professional.

You mean no malice; you mean no insult by it. You simply need to fix the mess of words placed in front of you.

SOFTWARE AND COMPUTER THINGS

You may have noticed that I am not mentioning any specific programs as I write this. That's because I want this book to be timeless, and effective, no matter when you might read it. Software and companies go away—and there will always be new things on the market.

So, I won't be specific here, but I would be remiss to not mention editing and proofing software in a book going over self-editing.

And they are worth mentioning. They are useful and effective tools.

They are not a replacement for your judgment in self-editing. You must never blindly accept the changes suggested by the software because it is not a perfect system and will not spot everything.

The other thing of note is that you cannot just rely on one of them. It's a very risky proposition to use only one software for your book. A single software will not catch nearly enough. I recommend at least two, and up to five if you can find that many and can use them within your budget.

You must mess around and experiment with them, however, to figure out what order to do them in, and which ones you trust. Some software will contradict another software, and then you have to decide which one you do not like, or which one is right.

No easy way to do this, either. It's just up to you to decide.

On that note, software like that can help with more than grammar. Though I was dubious and annoyed by it at first, a lot of them really can make my writing a lot clearer and easy to read. You need not use all the options and settings for such things, but they are worth exploring and using the settings that make sense for your style.

I love technology and believe that you should use the tools that do work. Being a writer is often a lonely and chaotic endeavor with a lot of spinning plates. Anything you can get help with is worth the effort.

So, use it, but don't *rely* on it. Use it, but don't let it make all your writing decisions for you.

YOUR EAR IS A BETTER EDITOR THAN YOUR EYES

I have tried, so often, to skip this step. Because it is a step that, if you are of a certain disposition, can and will drive you up the wall.

I am of that disposition, but I cannot argue with the results...so, here we are.

Use software to listen to your story. Let it play to you as an audiobook.

You would not believe the level of errors and issues and minor typos that can all be caught, faster, easier, and *cheaper*, by hearing the story you wrote aloud.

There are a few rules to this, though. I'll say each, then explain them one by one.

- Don't Over-Listen
- Momentum Loosens
- Grammar Is Not as Important as Flow

<u>Don't Over-Listen:</u>

It is easy to listen to the same sentence repeatedly and feel, deep in your core, there is something wrong with the wording there. That you are staring at a problem and simply cannot see it.

This may be true. Sometimes *there* is a problem, and you need to deal with it. It is even possible that every time you notice this, there is a problem. But that idea, thinking with that, acting on that, is a recipe for madness and frustration.

Perfectionism, uncertainty in writing ability, and fear of failure can easily color your hearing. If you can't find the issue after three times listening, then move on to the next sentence. Life is too short to look back that much.

Momentum Loosens:

If you do start and need to change something every few paragraphs, don't freak out right away. Momentum loosens this perfectionism. It reduces overthinking regarding word choices and such. After a solid hour, you will only hear the stuff that needs changing. It's weird to think about, but true: you have to get used to hearing your style.

It differs from having it come out of your fingers, hearing a voice say it, and that's okay and something to get used to.

Grammar Is Not as Important as Flow:

If it sounds right and communicates what you mean to say, then fuck grammar. Seriously. Grammar is a tool, and it is a tool that can be warped in very specific exceptions.

I stress you need to have good proficiency in words and grammar and have been self-editing for a while. But, once you are to a professional level: if something sounds right, but is not correct normally, grammatically, then you go with what sounds right.

This is dangerous advice to overuse, but it is advice that has meaning and a time when it is correct to employ.

It is a chore, it can be tedious, but listening to your work is the surest and cleanest way to get a good manuscript. Despite how it may seem, and despite most people reading books in their heads anyway, good writing will always sound good. Dialogue, prose, action scenes, doesn't matter.

Good writing sounds good, period.

THE FEAR OF THE PUBLISH

This is a classic piece of writing advice, but it will always hold: no book is ever done.

No book is free from errors.

No book will ever be what you want from it, not totally.

That is impossible. It should not be gone for or attempted.

Do not think you are the exception to this rule, and that with one more edit you can get every word perfect, and the story clean and shiny and revelatory.

You cannot.

You will not.

Stop fucking trying to make a book perfect.

The rules are simple, and horrible for nerves. Make a book as good as you can in a reasonable time. Throw all you have in the attempt. But be ready to publish and be ready to let it go and see what others think.

With some glaring exceptions, you can always write a new book. You will be writing new books. You will learn something new from each time you write a new book. You will learn a hell of a lot from each time you edit, and you will learn something akin to life lessons with each book published.

I know it's scary, but it is necessary. It is needed, and it is what you are here to do.

So, publish it and then get to the next one.

And, a final word of warning: don't go back.

Don't look back at the book you wrote. Once you publish it, once you have released it, don't go back and read it.

Only if you need to for a sequel should you ever look. And even then, a World Bible should be able to help you with that without opening the book again.

You will find something you don't like in the old book. You might even see something that will make you panic and fear that someone will discover you have no idea what you are doing.

Don't do that to yourself. Just let it be for others to read.

You wrote it for them, didn't you?

You have more important things to do then read your old stuff. Like writing another book.

Assignment 4:

Once I teach you this part, you should be in a manic but very productive game of swinging back and forth. Writing new books and then editing the old ones. You should be piling up books ready for publishing at a volume higher than you ever believed possible.

In one year, you will already be prolific. Hell, in less than that, this could be your full-time job. It happens more often than you'd think.

But only if you can keep up the pace. Only if you can keep putting out books, learning business techniques, and learning how to sell copies.

Just remember that the best way to sell a book is to write another book—and give them both a good, genre-appropriate cover.

Like the last time, I am going to basically be summarizing steps that should be clear from the articles—along with some fiddly bits.

1. Each day, as far separate from the writing part of your day as possible, edit the oldest book you've written that you have not already edited. There are a few substeps. They are time specific.

    a. On the first day:

- i. Copy the chapter files and compile them into one big file. Label the file with the name of your book plus the word VS1.

- ii. Put the title in big, fancy letters at the top of the first page. I will allow you this one moment of procrastinating. Have fun making the title look nice.

- iii. Change the size and style of font to something that you would not mind looking at for long stretches of time. You can make the words very big if it will help you focus on them.

b. On the 2nd through 6th day:

- i. Read through the entire book, as fast as you can. If you are following the "read 20 pages a day rule" from my last book, this *does* count toward that reading. Make any changes you see needed and rewrite any sections you cannot figure out how to fix. You cannot linger in this step, there is much to do beyond it.

- ii. Once you've gone through, copy this new version (you're leaving old versions as backups if you need to find what you had written before) and label it "VS2."

c. For the next few days, depending on specifics:

    i. Each day run the entire manuscript through one checker you started using. Do them one at a time unless you can do multiple at once. Fix or ignore each marked error as you go. Run maybe some twice if the software suggests a drastic volume of changes the first time.

    ii. Once this is done, make a "VS3" that is a copy of the updated file.

d. For the next while:

    i. Each day listen to at least three of the chapters (do the math for specific needed amounts based on how many chapters you have) in whatever software you have to read the story back to you. Some word processors have this as a default feature. This can take a while each day, but if you only do a chapter a day, you are not going to get done in a month, and there will be a backlog.

    ii. Once this is done, make sure to—you should be doing this at every stage, but especially here—make a backup on some cloud server or external hard drive. You do not want to lose the thing you worked on for so long.

2. You now have a completed, lightly edited manuscript. It's time to have someone else look at it. May I suggest a paid editor? This may seem like too expedited of a process, but this is not a game where you have the time to wait and get it all shiny. Editing for high-level publishing is not something that can be allowed to drag out for too long. If there are other steps you feel are crucial, if you feel you must do something before you can consider a manuscript done, then go ahead. But this is a quick workable way to put out a good product.

3. Fix any changes suggested to you by your editor. Note that, when using an editor, there are many types of them, and they will do different things. I will not go and explain them all here—do your homework on which types are best for you and best for your manuscript. Look for experience, especially in your genre, and be prepared to get a lot of corrections.

4. If a lot is changed by having a developmental editor work on your stuff, go back over your manuscript with all the grammar checkers again and clean up anything that got messed up. You can also hire (and I recommend you do) a proofreader to do this.

And that's it. Sort of anyway. With these steps repeated over and over again, you can do a full book every month or so. You will build a body of work that will help make your advertising and marketing efforts more effective.

Now, there are a few things still to go over. I want you to only read the next section once you have gotten through the entire edit of one of your books.

This is partially because I want you to actually do the steps and not just skim this book, and partially because I also have something special in the next section.

If you're too tempted, I suppose you can read the next article, just to dispel any mystery. But here's the gist of why I am including it: I fucked up on my own journey, and I don't want you to make the same mistake.

This book is not only a compendium of things I've learned work but also a result of failure and learning from that failure.

I did not balance my editing with my writing. I did not publish as I went. I just focused on the writing aspect for *several years* and that damage is done.

The next article is me exploring (about 5 months before I wrote this book) what happened when I failed to do it the way I am outlining here. Read it—but only that one article until you're done with this assignment—and hopefully learn from my mistakes that led to me developing the methods in this book.

The rest of the final section before we wrap this sucker up is a smattering of things to think about as you go toward publishing your first book.

MY OWN PERSONAL WRITER'S BLOCK

Okay, honest here, I've written a lot. Over 20 books. Depending on how you count novellas, it's a lot more than that. For over 2 years, closer to 3, I wrote around 1500 words a day. That's over a million words.

But, as you've noticed, I've published 2 books. Seriously, only 2 things have made it through my processes and got done.

This is because I am slow and methodical about editing. I'm likely too much of a perfectionist about editing.

In a real sense, my future as an author depends on my ability to get out new books. It's how an author gets paid, yeah? It's how we *are* authors.

So, I had to make a change. I had to find something, in some form, that would make it faster for me to put out books.

It's also necessary for me as a creative person.

Because I stopped writing new books. Short stories, poems, articles, blog posts, all of that I kept at because that's more my main job—but no books. I have all these stories allowed to languish on my computer, unloved and unread. To make another book feels wrong, so I can't do it anymore. That's my block.

So, again, I must make these old stories happen. And without losing quality, either. I won't shovel out these half-finished things: they need my hands to sculpt them into the books they're meant to be.

And maybe, just maybe, I've found an iota of a way to do this. My latest book was done using this plan, this strategy—and it only took a few months to publish, once I got going.

But that's *still* not fast enough.

We live in a world of pulp authors, yet again. Publishing is moving fast, digitally—and if I want to play, I must change even more.

So, what is the point of this article? What am I saying?

I'm saying expect more books from me.

Expect a lot more of them.

That's the plan, anyway.

KEEP DOWN THE COST

Welcome to the business aspect of the job. You've read stuff by me that already covers the parts of a book that need the most attention, but I need to make a special point of it.

I need you to understand that a book is a curious beast. It is the ultimate balancing act of cost to outcome.

Because not paying enough and setting loose on the world a suboptimal product will result in your book being a waste of the money you do spend.

But, simultaneously, do you know how unlikely it is that you will make all your money back on the first book you publish?

Your backlist, your collection of written books, the more the merrier, is how you make money. One is nothing, ten is much more powerful.

So, you can't afford to dump a ton of money into the first or first few you do. Unless your very rich or don't care about profits.

But, for the rest of us, we need to make sure our money is going where it needs to go.

And you do this by isolating the most important aspects of the cost. Of everything you spend money on with the first few books, what matters the most?

I already told you, but I'll say it again: cover and editing.

But also formatting because that is a big visual aspect of a book. That, too, is a lynchpin for someone buying and reading your book.

Advertising is more effective the more books you have to sell. There is a benefit to spending a fair bit to make sure your first book has a satisfying and attention-grabbing release. But, understand if you go big to begin, you are fighting against obscurity and won't see much in the way of returns.

It's likely going to be a money sucker and not make you your money back—at least right now.

If you get readers salivating for the next book of yours, then first, good job, and second, get them *that* book right away.

So, for your quick reference, I'll list the hierarchy of costs you need to incur:

1. Cover
2. Editing
3. Formatting
4. Advertising

Remember, if you are in a financially bad spot, you will need to pay for your next book with the money you make in sales. The ultimate goal is to make enough to get a profit and have enough left over to publish again.

That can be a razor-edged endeavor, and you need to be smart about it. So, I'm not saying to be cheap—but understand that you are also running a business here, and the cost to produce *matters*.

If you are going to make your books cost money, then you will probably need to spend some upfront, and hope to earn it back.

So be smart about it. Keep down the cost.

GETTING STUFF OFF YOUR PLATE

I do not pretend to know what your situation is when you picked up this book and decided that you would embark on this adventure. Maybe you have been meaning to be a published author for a long time, and you wanted to finally take that step and do so with gusto. Maybe you are hoping this could be your career.

But, regardless of your reasoning for it, there is something that you will learn as a person who runs entire businesses, often by yourself:

Get shit off your plate as much as you can afford to.

You are one person who has to do all aspects of a project, and that will become very scattering, distracting, and frustrating.

You'll know when you've hit this point when you do not know how you could get more done each day.

So, what do you do?

The solution is to hire someone else when you can afford it.

That's the best choice.

If you find you're making enough money to get people to do aspects of your job, then *do that*. You will be the one to write books and make a lot of decisions—and not much else. The more you can get it to that aspect strictly, mostly, the smoother this will all feel.

I know you didn't start down this journey to be the guy just filling out spreadsheets and running advertisements. That's not the goal of any pro-author, or writer.

And, yeah, you will be filling out spreadsheets for a time. A long time likely. You have to pay your dues and do everything—even and especially the parts of the job you don't enjoy. The goal, though, should be to pay other people to do stuff for you.

So, remember that, and be extra monitoring of your book sales and average income.

Institute a support team sooner.

You don't have to hire a full-time employee, either. Freelancers are always an option.

You just need someone who can take the edge off of the random tasks you have to do.

After all, you're a writer.

If you're not writing, what is the point of this?

THE STUFF IN THE BOOK YOU PROBABLY FORGOT TO WRITE

If you are anything like me, then you likely do not think about the other stuff you need to put in a book besides the actual story.

So, here's a quick reminder of the fiddly bits you also need to write. All are short and you can likely write them in a fairly small window of time.

You also don't technically need to do these. If one or more of them does not feel right, then you can skip them.

1. Dedications:

This should be no more than a few sentences and should be to the point. If there is someone or a few people who absolutely must be thanked for this book you made, then this is the place where you thank them. Don't worry, you can thank them again in the Acknowledgments in more depth.

2. Note from The Author:

Got something you feel like the reader needs to know about the story before they read it? This is where that goes. I recommend this if your plot has some real-world connection you want to confirm.

3. Acknowledgments:

This is where you can spend several pages talking about whatever or whoever you feel like you need to give respect to for the creation of your book or your progress as an author. I've seen people thank the Christian God, their parents, and inspiring shows or movies in their acknowledgments. You can put whatever you want here—just be respectful of other people's privacy.

4. About the Author Page:

I do not know if there is a best way to do these. Just put info about yourself that will be memorable enough that a reader will recall your name and personality next time they need something to read. This is also a great place to mention or list other books you've written. If this book—the one you're writing this for—is in a series, include a list that tells them where they are in the series.

Again, these are all fairly short, but you'll need them before you (or someone else) formats the book.

Assignment 5:

At this point, you will need to do your research. I am designing this book to not be very time locked. I want it to be useful for someone who wants to write books twenty years in the future. Though who knows how changed the future will be from now?

So, I won't tell you what websites to go to for designers or editors. I won't have specific things to recommend—just a general outline of steps.

1. If you haven't already, make several files, one for each of the additional book aspects like Dedications and Acknowledgments.
2. Create a new copy of your document, label this one VS4, and add to it, in the places they go, the additional data. Make sure that your chapter headers are still where you intended them to be in the document.
3. Go through and ensure that all of your chapters are still the correct numbers. This is an easy thing to miss, so check for it as its own step.
4. Find and hire a formatter who is experienced with wherever you are planning to self-publish your book. There are different file types for different publishers, at least at time of writing. You have to do this before you hire anyone else. Formatting changes your page count. If you are planning to publish the book as a hardcover or paperback,

then you need to know the size so your cover designer can make you a correct spine size.

5. Find and hire a cover designer that has proven their ability to make genre-appropriate covers. Check that they are legally making you a new cover and not stealing or reusing an existing one. Make sure they have a license for the images to be used for commercial purposes. Finally, give them accurate measurements of your book. Give them time to do this—and do not rush them. It may throw off your publishing schedule, but a good cover designer is worth it. You will probably have to use the same designer for all books in the same series, so don't piss them off.

6. Save all the data you have for the book in one folder, and in an easy-to-find place on your computer. You'll not want to have to hunt around your files when you're ready to publish.

7. This is not a marketing book, but I would be remiss if I did not mention the need for you to market before you release your book. The first few weeks and months of a book release matter—and you want that to be the apex of the attention that your book gets. Just keep this in mind.

8. Set aside a few hours to publish your book. It always takes a little longer to do than you think it will.

And that, finally, is it. You published a book. Your first one in a hopefully long chain of them.

It's a big deal. If you feel mentally exhausted or almost sad, that's normal. The sheer stress of publishing never does seem to disappear, only become less acute. Take a day where you only do the minimum of these rules and habits I've demanded of you.

You don't get breaks—sorry.

But you do get a day or two where you just write new words, and edit some stuff, and don't think too hard about the whole thing.

There will be much more to think about, much more to learn.

So much more.

But you do deserve some respite.

Here, at the end, I only have a little more to tell you, and one more assignment to wrap up this book. Read it all.

ART IS SUBJECTIVE AND PEOPLE LIKE DIFFERENT STUFF

Not everyone will be a fan of you or your work.

You will probably get bad reviews, and someone may even insult you. It's happened to me, and it will probably happen to you.

It's never fun, and it can ruin your entire day.

Books contain the souls of their authors, however small a piece of it. And it will and can and does sting to have that judged.

But there's no way to handle it except to write another book and keep going. If you stop making art, then you are the one who is going to lose something—not the person who reviewed you poorly.

Art helps combat the darkness of the world.

So, please don't stop, even if you get bashed.

Just keep going. Try not to reread that bad review, and just get writing the next thing.

If the flaw the reviewer says you have is true, then the best way to fix it is to practice more and write more and get better as an author.

I cannot claim there will be no bad days, awful days, days of raging self-doubt.

But I never want that to stop you from making something new.

It has made too many quit as it is.

Assignment 6 and Beyond:

If you listened to me, then you have been reading this book over more than a month, slowly and in chunks.

It's been a long journey, eh?

I hope you are already finding yourself happier and motivated by what you've accomplished.

I want you to know that it is important work being artists. Sure, that may be tooting my own horn, but I think it is the responsibility of artists that have found some success to pass advice and motivation to the next generation.

Selfishness has no place in art.

Seek to make the world fuller of beauty and art than you found it, and your life will have contributed to the human race.

That is not just the domain of the artist. It is the domain of mothers, doctors, priests, and many others.

But the artist, above all, has that as a job.

So, do it with pride.

Do it in a way that spreads it far and wide and brings you stability where you can find it.

There is no shame in making money as you do. We live in a society that requires it, and, unless that changes, we need the money to make more art and live to do so.

If I did not need money, I would still do this—and I hope you would as well. But it's okay to want it as a byproduct.

With these final steps, I let you out into the world with powerful tools. Use them wisely, use them ethically, and use them with confidence.

I want you to be the artist you always wanted to be, and the artist the world will be helped by having.

1. Keep going. Don't lose the pattern and the rhythm. The steps are meant to be done forever, in repetition, or for as long as you can and desire to keep writing books.
2. Reread this entire book in as close to one sitting as possible. I went over a lot in this book and had a few rather information-dense sections. I want you to be sure you have internalized the information. So, read this book again.
3. Every single time you release a book available in physical form, buy one. Make a section on a shelf and place them all in it. I don't recommend opening them—you will find something in them you won't like anymore. But the pile/row itself, the physical sight of it, is something that will inspire, and, as it grows, show you just how far you've come.

4. Share what you've learned from this book with others, should they show interest. I do not mind if you lend your purchased copy around to others. Don't steal from me, of course, but I'd much rather more people have these methods than deny them to people who can't or won't buy the book. Making artists is more important than one or two missed sales.

Thank you for reading this. Thank you for trusting me. It matters a great deal that you have the right tools. I hope I have just started something for you that will change your life.

As I like to do with this series, I'll leave you with something important. I hope it helps get you through the harder times. I hope it makes it easier to strive for better and better futures.

The Motto of Immortality

(In the moments and on the days where there seems to be no hope anymore as an artist, say these things aloud or in your head, and believe them.)

Beauty outlasts everything.

The world will still have it even when all else is gone.

The sky will still blaze,

And the wind will still stir plants.

But now is the time when it needs it most.

Now is the time for creativity.

There's no one else who makes it the way I do.

And no one else will make it for me.

I was given an artistic drive for a reason.

I need not know the reason,

So long as I act upon it.

Even if only one soul beyond my own is helped,

Then what I made is worth it.

The world needs more art,

More songs, and stories, and light, and joy,

And it will always need more.

I will not lose the ability to make art,

And I will make it better always.

So long as there is joy, there can be art.

So long as there is art, there can still be joy.

So long as there is beauty, there can be hope for everything,

Everything in this massive cosmos.

While I may be a speck upon it,

That is also all we see of stars,

And we are made better for having their shine,

And we are better for having me to make art.

ABOUT THE AUTHOR

From a young age, Brandon Scott realized he was tired of stories where all the characters survived, and the good guys always won. And, after flirting off and on with the idea of writing for a few years, he got his first disturbed shudder out of a reader. Since then, Brandon Scott has been chasing that same shudder, penning dark speculative fiction stories of various lengths—some of which even he can't think about for too long without his stomach tightening.

When Brandon Scott is not writing, sleeping, cooking, or just busy with life stuff (a rare thing indeed) he enjoys anime, books, movies, television, dumb online videos, and really anything you might call "nerdy" or "geeky." He lives in Florida and somehow still manages to feel cold.

Printed in Great Britain
by Amazon